What's the Word?

What's the Word?

Teresa Sheppard

Gathered Publishing

CONTENTS

CONTENTS

Words have energy and power with the ability to help, to heal, to hinder, to hurt, to harm, to humiliate, and to humble. Words are the most powerful force available to humanity. Words can build; words can tear down. That is why I challenge you to ask God to give you a word for the year. I promise you will be amazed at how that word will influence your life during the year.

One year my word was "Soar" and my verse was Isaiah 40:31 "but those who trust in the Lord will renew their strength; they will soar on wings like eagles; they will run and not grow weary; they will walk and not faint." I loved the visual of the words in this verse—I wanted to soar! Before the year was over God, showed me that I could not soar because I was tethered. When I begin asking God to show me what I was tethered to, He showed me it was an un-forgiveness from a hurt that I had buried in my heart 10 years earlier never to think about it again. Yes, it was painful to face and to deal with but I did not want to be tethered; the thought of soaring above everything of this world was greater than the pain I knew I had to face. After several months of prayer, ugly crying, writing letters to the one who had hurt me and shredding them allowing those ugly words to appear on the paper but never allowing anyone to see them but God, forgiveness began to happen and what a feeling of freedom I experienced and then I began to Soar! God has given me many opportunities to share this experience as I minister to women in Faith Promise Church. I may never have had the opportunity to serve as Director of Faith Promise Stephen Ministry if I had not had this experience. I will forever be grateful that God gave me the word "Soar" for my word that year.

Believe me, you will never regret choosing a word for the year. That word begins to show up in so many places at the strangest time to get your attention. That word guides you, gives meaning, grows you, and glorifies Him.

Patsy Williams

Words are Powerful!

"Faith convinces us that God created the world through his word. This means that what can be seen was made by something that could not be seen." Hebrews 11:3 GWT

Our entire reality was created by words from God. Our words have power, too.

We find proof of that in the Bible.

"A gentle answer turns away rage,
but a harsh word stirs up anger." Proverbs 15:1 GWT

"A soothing tongue is a tree of life,
but a deceitful tongue breaks the spirit." Proverbs 15:4 GWT

"People who want to live a full life and enjoy good days must keep their tongues from saying evil things and their lips from speaking deceitful things." 1 Peter 3:10 GWT

"What goes into a person's mouth doesn't make him unclean. It's what comes out of the mouth that makes a person unclean." Matthew 15:11 GWT

The scriptures above are a few examples of the power of our words. The Bible goes even further than that.

"From the fruit of a man's mouth his stomach is satisfied; he is satisfied by the yield of his lips. Death and life are in the power of the tongue, and those who love it will eat its fruits." Proverbs 18:20-21 ESV

LIFE AND DEATH are in the power of the tongue!

How do our words have power?

"I will do anything you ask the Father in my name so that the Father will be given glory because of the Son. If you ask me to do something, I will do it." John 14:13-14 GWT

Our words have power because Jesus will do anything, we ask in His name. There is nothing more powerful than God.

Jesus told the wind to stop, and the dead to rise. All were amazed at the power He had. He gave us power through the Holy Spirit.

"I can guarantee this truth: Those who believe in Me will do the things that I am doing. They will do even greater things because I am going to the Father." John 14:12 GWT

Words are powerful!

Word of the Year

The word of the year is a word that you choose and meditate on all year long. You should also choose a scripture that goes along with that word.

Does the Bible tell you to have a "Word" for the year? No. It doesn't spell that out. We ask God to show us a word that He wants us to focus on because it is a foundation that guides us into God's will for the year. Meditating on God's word and will is biblical.

Do you normally plan where you are going before you get in your car? Usually, right? Having a word for the year could be compared to setting a destination.

How about you?
Have you had a word of the year before?

If yes, what was it?

What was the scripture that went with it?

Can you think of ways that you saw evidence of the word manifest?

If so, what happened?

Examples

Examples

The Bible says that faith comes by hearing. I suppose we learn a lot of things by example. The Bible tells us to be an example to others. This book is written to guide you into your word and into harnessing the power of it. It may help you to see examples of words and scriptures that others have chosen.

*Remember, you can choose any word and any scripture as the Holy Spirit leads you. These are just given as a point of reference.

Joy:

"You will go out with joy and be led out in peace. The mountains and the hills will break into songs of joy in your presence, and all the trees will clap their hands." Isaiah 55:12 GWT

(This has been a great word for 2020. A reminder that Joy comes from the Lord and isn't dependent upon circumstances or feelings.)

Prophecy:

"On the other hand, the one who prophesies speaks to people for their upbuilding and encouragement and consolation." 1 Corinthians 14:3 ESV

(This scripture seems like it could be a definition of Christian caregiving)

Prayer:

"Then you will call to Me. You will come and pray to Me, and I will hear you. When you look for Me, you will find Me. When you wholeheartedly seek Me," Jeremiah 29:12-13 GWT

(Don't we all need to be reminded that God will come to us when we pray.)

Thanksgiving:

"Give thanks in all circumstances; for this is the will of God in Christ Jesus for you." 1 Thessalonians 5:18 ESV

(We can all be spoiled children at times. Jesus taught the importance of thankfulness. See Luke 17:11-19)

Ideas?
Is your mind filling with ideas?

Ask the Lord what your word and your scripture for next year is. The spirit will show you.

Write your notes here:

What's the Word?

What is the word the Lord showed you?

What scriptures can you find that are related to the word?

Why do you feel led to this word?

It is okay if you don't know. It is even okay if God reveals something completely unexpected to you. I chose Joy for 2020. Then I asked God, "Did I hear wrong?" It sure felt like I got it wrong. I didn't have it wrong. God gave me that word to remind me that my joy comes from Him. It is not subject to what is going on around me.

Monthly Reflections

January

Word:

Scripture:

How have you meditated on your word and scripture this month?

What have you noticed as a result?

February

Word:

Scripture:

How have you meditated on your word and scripture
this month?

What have you noticed as a result?

March

Word:

Scripture:

How have you meditated on your word and scripture this month?

What have you noticed as a result?

April

Word:

Scripture:

How have you meditated on your word and scripture
this month?

What have you noticed as a result?

May

Word:

Scripture:

How have you meditated on your word and scripture
this month?

What have you noticed as a result?

June

Word:

Scripture:

How have you meditated on your word and scripture
this month?

What have you noticed as a result?

July

Word:

Scripture:

How have you meditated on your word and scripture
this month?

What have you noticed as a result?

August

Word:

Scripture:

How have you meditated on your word and scripture this month?

What have you noticed as a result?

September

Word:

Scripture:

How have you meditated on your word and scripture
this month?

What have you noticed as a result?

October

Word:

Scripture:

How have you meditated on your word and scripture
this month?

What have you noticed as a result?

November

Word:

Scripture:

How have you meditated on your word and scripture
this month?

What have you noticed as a result?

December

Word:

Scripture:

How have you meditated on your word and scripture this month?

What have you noticed as a result?

.

6

Looking Back

How do you feel God spoke through your word?

Do you think it helped having a word and scripture
to focus on?

What is something memorable that happened relating
to your word and scripture?

What is your word for next year?

What is the scripture(s)?

7

Looking Ahead

What is your word for next year?

What scripture(s) go with it?

Why do you feel led to that word?

Made in the USA
Columbia, SC
29 November 2020